TEACHING OLDER ADULTS

Linda Jane Vogel

Creative Teaching and Learning Series

DISCIPLESHIP RESOURCES
MATERIALS FOR GROWTH IN CHRISTIAN FAITH AND LIFE
P.O. Box 189 • Nashville, TN 37202 • Phone (615) 340-7285

Unless otherwise indicated, all scripture quotations are taken from the Revised Standard Version of the Holy Bible.

ISBN 0-88177-063-9

Library of Congress Catalog Card No. 88-72384

TEACHING OLDER ADULTS. Copyright © 1989 by Linda Jane Vogel. All rights reserved. Printed in the United States of America. No part of this book may be reproduced in any manner whatsoever without written permission, except in the case of brief quotations embodied in critical articles or reviews. For information, address Discipleship Resources Editorial Offices, P. O. Box 840, Nashville, TN 37202.

DR063B

To

my mother and dad
Gladys and Marvin Hutson
who model creative learning
in later life

Contents

Introduction *vii*

1. A Gold Mine of Lived Experience 1
   Gifts Older Adults Bring 1
   Needs Older Adults Bring 2

2. Getting Inside God's Word with Older Adults 5
   Ways We Experience Scripture 5
   The Bible and Our Life Journey 7
   Encountering the Gospel Story 8

3. Invitational Teaching 11
   Starting Where We Are 11
   Stories Meeting Gospel Story 14
   Faith-Sharing That Invites Commitment 16

4. Teaching/Learning with Older Adults 21
   Planning Learning Experiences 21
   Creating a Learning Environment 22
   Teaching Tools for Growing Christians 23
   Evaluation 28

5. Planning to Teach 31
   Teachers of Older Adults 31
   An Overview of Curriculum Resources 32
   Developing a Teaching Plan 35

Conclusion 41

Notes 43

Bibliography 47

Introduction

How can we share our faith and invite older adults to share their faith as we study and grow together in the church? How can we help persons identify and name their experiences as they work to make meaning of their lives? How can we join with them in seeking to make and strengthen our faith commitments?

We will explore these questions as we focus on teaching older adults in the church. We will explore the meaning of "invitational teaching" and consider some practical ways teachers can teach so that older adults grow in faith.

The Christian church has grown because people who knew Jesus Christ as their Savior invited others to join with them in this faith journey. Jesus called twelve disciples and eventually sent seventy persons out to spread the good news of God's love for all persons. This good news captured the imagination of many persons in the first century. It was too good to keep, and it spread beyond the Jewish community into the Gentile community. For almost two thousand years, the Christian church has been growing and spreading around the world. Today, persons who have experienced God's forgiving and empowering love are called to invite others to become disciples of Jesus Christ.

Older persons bring rich and varied life experiences to their exploration of the meaning of life and death in the context of Christian faith. They also bring a great deal of baggage—some hurts and misconceptions about the church and faith. There can be no more rewarding task than to engage in creative teaching/learning with these persons.

Our goal is to inspire and challenge those who teach in the church. We will explore new ways to teach for commitment, while respecting the opinions and decisions of every student. It is hoped that the information and suggestions that follow will help teachers engage in educational ministry with, by, and for older adults, so that both teachers and learners will grow in wisdom and knowledge and in the assurance that God loves them.

1
A Gold Mine of Lived Experience

Generalizing is dangerous. Being old means many different things. Persons face widely divergent physical, psychological, and social circumstances; and they cope in many and varied ways.

Nevertheless, persons in the last third of the life span (those 55 and older) are survivors. To a greater or lesser degree, they have managed to face the ups and downs, the good and the bad, as they have lived life. It has been said that older persons are the greatest natural resource our nation has.

GIFTS OLDER ADULTS BRING

Years of experience in weighing alternatives, making choices, and working out the consequences of their choices provide older adults with a vast array of resources to aid them in facing the future. Most older persons have experienced some significant losses (e.g., loss of spouse, job, health); and dealing with such losses has necessitated their developing coping skills. These skills are gifts that must be treated with care and respect.

Not all older persons are wise, but wisdom and understanding often grow out of facing life with its joys and frustrations, its challenges and disappointments. When persons "name" what they have learned, they may uncover gifts they did not know they had. Validating past experiences and discerning how growth has resulted often leads to increased wisdom and understanding.

Today's older adults have experienced more change at a faster rate than any preceding generation. Many of these persons have seen the horse and buggy replaced by the Model T; they have driven big, fast cars and small, economical cars; they have seen the trains come and go; they have watched a man take the first step on the moon! They can remember when people routinely died of pneumonia; they can recall the miracle of penicillin. Now they are confronted by the threat of nuclear annihilation and the AIDS epidemic. They remember when wages for a week were less than what many people make in an hour today!

Older adults may have experienced a time when the church was the social center of the community. They remember a time when it took weeks to hear what was happening in the world outside their doors; now they experience what is happening around the world—and even in outer space—while sitting in their own living rooms!

These elders among us marveled at the ballpoint pen; now they wonder at the complexities of computers! Automation, new roles for women and men, commuter marriages, and myriad other lifestyle options must be mind-boggling.

Today's older adults have seen and done more than most young people can imagine! Their ability to cope with an ever-changing world provides them with stories to tell and gifts to share. All who open themselves to share with older adults are bound to be enriched!

Survival skills, wisdom, and understanding are gifts which enrich the teaching/learning environment. They need to be valued, fostered, and built upon, so that—together—learners and teachers can grow in faith.

NEEDS OLDER ADULTS BRING

"Do not cast me off in the time of old age; forsake me not when my strength is spent."

(Psalm 71:9)

Both strength and needs grow from losses. Questions such as the following can help persons deal with the needs:

What is it that you need to keep your life together? Where are you hurting?

One community decided that it wanted to discover the needs of older persons and find ways to respond to those needs. The Shepherd's Center began in Kansas City in response to a congregation's belief that it needed to find ways to minister to older adults in the community.[1] The story of its birth is fascinating: What persons thought older adults needed (housing) differed from what study and listening showed that they really did need. As the Shepherd's Center has grown and developed, it has provided a model for congregations and communities throughout the United States.

The model provides a way of organizing the needs of older adults. Whatever needs exist for persons in your group, it may be helpful to organize them using the Shepherd's Center categories:

Life maintenance needs are those basic human needs that all persons must have met to survive—nutritious meals, health care, shelter, adequate financial resources, transportation.

Life enrichment needs are met when persons acquire coping and life-enriching skills that allow them to maintain their maximum level of independent living. An emphasis on wellness and an engagement in meaningful activities often result when these needs are met.

Life reconstruction needs arise whenever persons experience significant losses. How does one manage after the death of a spouse or a child? What does one do when one loses a job or has to give up a lifelong home? What does divorce or the loss of siblings and peers require of one? How can one handle physical or mental losses?

Life transcendence needs surface when persons seek to participate in the mysteries of life and to make sense of their own life and death in the larger scheme of things. Some significant questions grow out of these life transcendence needs with which persons in the last third of the life span often wrestle. The church can provide an appropriate setting for struggling with questions and issues, such as:

> Who am I?
> How can I continue to be a contributing and valued member of society?
> How can I assume responsibility for and feel good about (or at least accept) the choices I have made?
> What is the meaning of (my) life and death?

Addressing the needs that older adults face can be a challenging and rewarding opportunity. There is, indeed, a gold mine of experience and wisdom to be treasured and enhanced. There are barriers and pitfalls to overcome. Those who choose to share their lives and to be entrusted with the lives of older adults will be blessed!

2
Getting Inside God's Word with Older Adults

The Bible is the church's book. The Bible is the Word of God; but, most important, the Bible is God's Word *for you* and *for me!* Our goal is to join with older persons as we seek to experience the "holy" and to enter into dialogue with the biblical text. The Bible story needs to become *our story!*

As we help persons encounter God's Word for them, the Bible becomes a living book. The Holy Spirit engages us and empowers us to grow in faith and in love for God and for our sisters and brothers, who are *all* God's children.

WAYS WE EXPERIENCE SCRIPTURE

The Bible is a library of sixty-six books. It contains stories and history, hymns and poetry, laws and liturgies, letters and sermons. It is a record of God's acts in history as God called and judged and nurtured and forgave Abraham and Sarah and all their descendants. It is a record of the experiences of individuals and of the Israelites—God's chosen people—as they encountered the living God.

The Bible gives us accounts of the life and teachings of Jesus; it witnesses to Jesus' death and resurrection; it helps us understand the early beginnings of the church.

It is possible to "learn" about the Bible. We can discover how and when and by whom it was written; we can master the content. This is certainly an important task and one which deserves to be done.

However, our intent now is to help persons *experience* the world of the Bible and God's Word to all of us. We want to provide a setting and a method that invites older adults to enter into the lives and teachings recorded in the Bible. We want older adults to "feel with" (empathize), to identify with the struggles, to experience the valleys and the peaks of the persons in the Bible stories.

We can do this by following some simple guidelines.[1]

Help persons "feel into" the text. You might include activities, such as drama, role-playing, or music.

Help persons "meet with" the text so that they become involved in it. Dorothy Jean Furnish describes meeting with the text as an experience that provides us with a snapshot that captures a particular event or experience. Films, videos, hymns, and storytelling are tools that can help persons "meet with" the Bible's story.

Finally, *we need to encourage persons to "respond out of" their encounter with the biblical text.* Doing so will involve persons intellectually and affectively. We need to think, discuss, decide, and act, as we internalize and make the Bible story our own story.

For example, if your group were studying the account of Jesus feeding the five thousand (John 6), you might use a guided meditation that helps persons put themselves in that time and place to encourage them to "feel into" the text. Richard J. Foster[2] suggests that we ask persons to identify with someone in the Bible story: the boy who shared his lunch, one of the disciples, or perhaps someone on the edge of the crowd.

Set the stage by saying that it must have been spring, because the grass was green and it was near the time of Passover. Help persons feel the grass and the warm earth. Ask them to listen to the sounds—the lapping of the water against the shore and the murmuring of the crowd. Urge them to feel the hardness of the rocks on which they sit, the coarseness of their clothes, the closeness of the people around them. Encourage the group to empathize with those in the story: What emotions wash over them? Hesitancy to share? Amazement? Joy?

Once you have set the stage, slowly read John 6:1-13. Following the reading, Foster suggests we say something like this:

Then, in your imagination, watch the crowd leave and Jesus go up into the hills. You are left alone. You sit on a rock overlooking the water and reexperience the events of the day. You become quiet, and after a little while, Jesus returns and sits on a nearby rock. For a time, you are both silent, looking out over the water perhaps and enjoying one another's presence. After a bit, the Lord turns to you and asks the question, "What may I do for you?" Then you tell him what is in your heart—your needs, your fears, your hopes....

When you have finished, you become quiet for a little while. Then you turn to the Lord and ask, "What may I do for you?" And you listen, with the heart quietly, prayerfully....[3]

When using guided imagery, allow persons time to open their eyes and come back to the present.

Once you have helped persons "feel into" the text, encourage them to "meet with" the text. Persons might want to share some of what they have experienced. Look at the text from the points of view of the disciples, the boy who shared, a skeptic in the crowd, and Jesus. The feeding of the five thousand is the only miracle story that is found in all four Gospels. Have persons look at the accounts in Matthew, Mark, and Luke. Afterward, ask: "What does this story mean for us today? What are we called to be and do?" Our task as teachers is to help the persons we teach "respond out of" their encounter with the biblical text.

THE BIBLE AND OUR LIFE JOURNEY

How many times have you encountered a startling new idea only to be informed, "I've told you that before!"? Many insights go right by us—that is, until that "teachable moment," when we need them to help us make sense of our situation. Then they "grab us," and we are able to internalize them.

Teaching older adults ought to involve us in helping persons see their own lives in light of the good news (gospel) of Jesus Christ. It ought to lead to an understanding and a transformation of our actions, beliefs, and values.

Our starting points, then, are the life situations of the learners. Each learner brings his or her own life experience—joys and pains, successes and failures, inner resources and losses.

As brothers and sisters of faith, we need to join together on a faith pilgrimage, where we listen to and care for one another. Study the Bible together. Have someone read a Bible passage that relates to the issues and concerns of persons in your group; then ask the group to consider these three questions:

(1) What did you hear?
(2) What did you see?
(3) What did you feel?

These questions seem simple, and they are; but you will be amazed at how these questions open up the meaning of scripture in personal ways. The "stories" of older adults suddenly and meaningfully may be seen in light of the larger story of the gospel. This approach works especially well with older adults, because they have so much life experience to draw upon as they seek new ways of understanding God's Word for them.

ENCOUNTERING THE GOSPEL STORY

As we bring the stories of persons in the group and *The Story* of the good news of Jesus Christ into dialogue, we gain new insights and discover alternative actions. The biblical story, which has been preserved by believers over two-thousand years, can lead us to discover new meanings and insights, to grow in understanding and trust, and to act in new ways.

The gospel story enables older adults to explore meanings in life and to wrestle with questions of integrity that are characteristic of persons in old age. Such exploration can lead to an increased sense of personal meaning and integrity.

By struggling with questions of life and death in the light of the gospel, older persons may be able to say "yes" to the good and the bad in their lives and to move toward a deeper sense of peace and wholeness. New meanings of self-worth and self-acceptance may emerge, leading toward being more accepting of those who are different.

Questions that may be explored as individual stories and visions intersect the Judeo-Christian Story and Vision include:

> Why must I (or my loved one) die?
> What is the meaning to be found in our suffering?
> What use am I now that I am so dependent?
> Is there any good that can come out of the losses I am experiencing?
> Why must I live, when I have nothing to live for?

The good news of Jesus Christ is that God loves us and forgives us. We are valuable to God because we were created by God. Nothing is so evil or so powerful that it can separate us from the love of God through Christ Jesus—"neither death nor life, neither angels nor other heavenly rulers or powers, neither the present nor the future... there is nothing in all creation that will ever be able to separate us from the love of God which is ours through Christ Jesus our Lord" (Romans 8:38-39).

An encounter with the gospel story that involves older adults in "feeling into," "meeting with," and "responding out of" the biblical story has great potential for helping persons grow as disciples of Jesus Christ. The Bible story can become *our story*. When it does, we have—in fact—experienced the "holy"!

3
Invitational Teaching

Invitational teaching is nothing new. In fact, it dates at least to the time of Joshua! After Joshua led the Israelites into the promised land, we are told that he gathered all the tribes of Israel together at Shechem. In a powerful farewell address before he died, Joshua reminded the people of all that God had done and was doing for them. Then he said, "Choose this day whom you will serve...but as for me and my house, we will serve the Lord" (Joshua 24:15). The prophets continued this tradition and were often "invitational" in their teaching and preaching.

Jesus' teaching often invited people to grow and change. He used stories and asked penetrating questions. Jesus always respected the backgrounds and beliefs of his hearers. He began where they were; and he used dialogue, stories, and questions to help them confront new possibilities. Jesus helped persons see things in more inclusive and less judgmental ways.

STARTING WHERE WE ARE

Have you ever been in a class where the vocabulary or the concepts or the skills required to do a task were beyond your experience? Like me, you probably threw your hands up in frustration and said, "This is beyond me! I quit!" You may even have felt, "I'm not smart enough to do this," or "I'm too old to learn new things!"

I have good news for all who have had this experience! You are not too old, and you are smart enough! The problem is not *you!* The problem is that the experience was designed for persons at a different level of development, knowledge, or skill.

All of us who teach in the church need to remember what

it is like to find ourselves in that kind of situation. We need to avoid doing to others what has been done to us!

The first requirement for teaching older adults is *to know the persons you teach*. Sharing backgrounds and getting acquainted is not "an extra" or a waste of time. It is absolutely essential if we are to teach invitationally.

What are the accomplishments, the hopes, and the dreams of the persons you teach? What are their fears? What disappointments and losses have they experienced?

What experiences have they had with education and with the church? Do they feel good about themselves and optimistic about the future, or are they fearful? Do they feel inadequate? Are they willing to share and risk, or are they afraid of judgment and failure?

But please note: I am NOT suggesting that you begin your first session by asking questions such as these!

Invitational teaching *provides opportunities* for persons to share as much or as little as they are comfortable doing. It *opens doors;* it *models* what can happen when persons risk sharing their hopes and fears.

Invitational teaching *respects the right of persons to share or not, as they choose*. Finally, invitational teaching needs to be done in an atmosphere of trust, where persons covenant together to *hold in confidence* what persons share with the group—their hopes and joys, hurts and fears.

We must be sensitive to the developmental tasks of older adults. Persons such as Abraham Maslow, Erik Erikson, Robert Peck, Roger Gould, and Howard McClusky offer us insights here.[1]

Clearly, we need to be aware of the needs persons have at all levels. The Shepherd's Center model organizes needs according to categories of life maintenance, life enrichment, life reconstruction, and life transcendence. Howard McClusky uses these categories: coping needs, expressive needs, contributive needs, influence needs, and the need for transcendence.[2]

McClusky has developed a formula that can help us understand those with whom we work. He suggests that if we are aware of the strengths and resources individuals have at their disposal, and if we put these over against the internal and external demands made on them that require energy and may result in stress, then we can better assess the margin they have to invest in learning.

McClusky's formula is called the PLM Teaching/Learning Model: *P*ower divided by *L*oad yields *M*argin.[3]

$$\frac{POWER}{LOAD} = MARGIN$$

Whenever persons have more demands (*L*oad) being made on their lives than they have resources (*P*ower) for dealing with those demands, then they have no margin (*M*) to invest in learning—even if they really need new information or coping skills. The PLM model can help us be sensitive to persons whom we believe we could help, but who—for some reason—resist or are not receptive to our teaching/learning endeavors.

Evelyn and James Whitehead write about an inner strength that may come as persons age and mature. These authors believe that, in late adulthood, it is possible and desirable for persons to reflect on and evaluate their lives. Questions of meaningfulness or absurdity, wholeness or negation, affirmation or despair can be examined and resolved.[4] This process can lead to greater maturity as older persons examine their lives.

It is important to discover the gifts and needs of learners and to listen to their questions and to their life stories as they share them. Teachers need to be willing to share their own journeys and needs in appropriate ways. Recognizing that older persons will be at many different places on their pilgrimages and that teachers and students alike can listen and learn from one another is essential.

Respect and acceptance of each person's spiritual development is a key. We need to recognize that we cannot give our "answers" to others; instead, we are called to listen and care for persons as they engage in their own struggles to find answers for themselves.

STORIES MEETING GOSPEL STORY

Let us reflect together on several scenarios where groups of older adults have come together to participate in a teaching and learning experience in the church. Ask yourself: "How can individuals' stories intersect with the gospel story, so that persons will grow in faith and love and experience more fully the grace of God in their lives?"

A group of widows, who had recently lost their husbands, came together to form a *Grief and Loss Sharing Group*. The load (L) they were carrying was great. Several of the women did not drive, and their husbands' deaths meant a loss of independence and mobility. Some had never taken care of financial matters. Several had known deeply fulfilling relationships, while others were experiencing both loss and a newfound freedom.

The leader or facilitator of this group was a good listener. She understood the grief process and the value of discovering that others share similar feelings—whether those are feelings of loneliness or feelings of guilt, feelings of helplessness or feelings of anger. She recognized the importance of having group members help set the agenda of the group. She tried to create an atmosphere where persons would be accepted, no matter what level of participation (or nonparticipation) they chose.

The group began by getting better acquainted. As they introduced themselves, they shared as much of their personal stories and losses as they chose.

The leader then shared a couple of verses from Matthew's Gospel—at the beginning of the account of Jesus feeding the five thousand. Most of the group members were familiar with the story, but few remembered the context. The leader asked the group to recall that John the Baptist, Jesus' cousin and friend, had just been put to death by Herod. The group members read Matthew 14:12-13*a* aloud and reflected on what may have been going through Jesus' mind. How might he have felt? Are there times when we want to have time alone?

Invitational Teaching

The group's discussion of Jesus' grief led to a discussion of their own grief. Experiencing grief is a healthy, good thing. It enables us to work through the losses we have suffered. Knowing that Jesus, too, must have experienced grief can be reassuring.

As a new sharing group begins, they will find much comfort in the Psalms and in Habakkuk 1:2: "O Lord, how long shall I cry for help, and thou wilt not hear?" Discovering that many times in the Bible persons cried out in despair or in anger at God can be a freeing experience.

This is not the time to focus on those great passages of victory (for example, Romans 8), though that time will come. When persons are weighed down with grief, God's Word to them is that they are not alone in their grief! God cares about them and can understand and accept them with their feelings of anger or frustration or despair.

Another group of older adults in a downtown congregation expressed interest in serious Bible study. "I am tired," one woman said, "of sitting around sharing what we each think some passage means!" Her group was ready to encounter hard questions growing out of an informed understanding of the background and insights of biblical scholarship. Such questioning could further inform their own reading of the gospel.

A diaconal minister secured the RSV Video Bible study on the Gospel of Mark and went to work.[5] In that video, four New Testament scholars from different backgrounds and perspectives helped the group focus on major themes in Mark's Gospel. Every one of the thirteen class members read the assignment before each meeting and struggled with the questions to be tackled. They reflected on Jesus' acceptance of and advocacy for the powerless; they tried to look at their own church and community to discover what it would mean for them to work actively to re-order the power structures of which they were a part.

Seeking to understand who and what Jesus Christ is as he is portrayed in Mark's Gospel led them to examine who and what Jesus Christ is in their lives today. They struggled with the role of women and Jesus' attitude and actions toward them in Mark; they tried to discern what this meant for them and their attitudes toward women today.

Biblical scholars as they came to the group on videotape, Bible, commentaries, a study guide, and the members' own questions and insights yielded a dynamic and growth-producing study.

A third example of stories meeting *Gospel Story* is a small group of older men who met to study the United Methodist Bishops' pastoral letter on peace, "In Defense of Creation." These men came from varied backgrounds and were politically diverse. Several were veterans who believe that peace is best attained through a strong national defense. One was strongly committed to stopping the arms race. All were seeking to be faithful disciples of Jesus Christ.

The men agreed to come together to pray and to study the background document which came with the Bishops' pastoral letter. They agreed at the outset that they would *listen* to one another, but that they would not try to convert others to their own points of view. They agreed to *love and accept* one another as brothers in Christ, even though they might differ on what it means to be faithful regarding nuclear issues and a just peace.

The men took turns leading the group. They always began with Bible study, but they agreed that they would not try to "prove their points" with the Bible.

The group members were willing to *risk* encountering the living Word of God and to be open to the guidance of the bishops of their church as they struggled with an issue of life or death for future generations—perhaps for the world.

FAITH-SHARING THAT INVITES COMMITMENT

"Tell me the stories of Jesus, I love to hear..." begins an old gospel hymn. The story of Jesus and of God's love for all persons is a story that we are called to share. It is a story people are hungry to hear.

The Bible instructs us to share our faith. An Old Testament passage that makes this clear is Deuteronomy 6:1-9. The commandments are commended to the people—"As long as you live, you and your descendants are to have reverence for the Lord your God and obey all [his] laws that I am giving you, so that you may live in that land a long time. Listen to them, people of Israel, and obey them!" The laws are summed up in this great commandment: "Israel, remember this! The Lord—and the Lord alone—is our God. Love the Lord your God with all your heart, with all your soul, and with all your strength. *Never forget these commands* that I am giving you today. *Teach them to your children.* Repeat them when you are at home and when you are away, when you are resting and when you are working. Tie them on your arms and wear them on your foreheads as a reminder. Write them on the doorposts of your houses and on your gates" (Deuteronomy 6:1-9, TEV).

Jesus called the twelve; and after living with them and instructing them, after showing them what it meant to be loved and forgiven by God, Jesus sent them out to spread God's love for all persons (Matthew 10:5-15; Mark 6:7-13; Luke 9:1-6). In Luke 10:1-12, we read about Jesus sending out another seventy persons in pairs to heal and teach.

After Jesus' crucifixion and resurrection and just before the ascension, Jesus proclaims, "I have been given all authority in heaven and on earth. Go, then, to all peoples everywhere and make them my disciples; baptize them in the name of the Father, the Son, and the Holy Spirit, and teach them to obey everything I have commanded you. And I will be with you always, to the end of the age" (Matthew 28:18*b*-20, TEV).

Still, the disciples were uncertain about their task. However, with the coming of the Holy Spirit at Pentecost, their uncertainty was transformed into power to proclaim the good news of Jesus Christ. And three thousand people were baptized that day (Acts 2:41). From that day to the present, disciples of Jesus Christ are called to share the good news of the gospel.

Sharing the good news is a commission we cannot avoid; yet, we often hesitate to speak of our faith. Some, reacting against experiences that had offended them, claim they will let their actions speak for them. Certainly, our actions must be consistent with the gospel if what we say is to be credible; but many good persons show compassion for others. We are called to name the name of Jesus—the one in whose name and for whose sake, we show acts of love and compassion. Doing and saying must go hand in hand!

Another error Christians sometimes make is to assume that Christian commitment is a once for all event. Rocky Smith, long-time teacher at Garrett-Evangelical Theological Seminary, used to say: "The trouble with testimony meetings is that people stand up and tell what Jesus did for them ten or fifty years ago when they were saved! What we are called on to share is what Jesus is doing in our lives yesterday and today—right now!"

If we want to be invitational teachers, we have to risk telling our own stories. We have to be willing to say what God is doing in our lives—now! We need to identify with persons and events in the biblical record and be willing to identify our own "burning bush" and our own "wrestling until daybreak with God." We need to share those experiences where we have felt abandoned by God—like Hosea and Jeremiah, or like Jesus on the cross. We need to share our church struggles and disagreements in light of the struggles between Peter and Paul in the early church.

Learning to speak the language of faith and to communicate empathy and our commonality with our sisters and brothers of the faith in the Bible is a key to invitational teaching. We need to invite others to "accept Jesus as their Savior" or to "become disciples of Jesus Christ."

Why is it that we sometimes hesitate to invite persons to become a part of our family of faith, when we so easily invite them to join our bowling league or to try a favorite restaurant or see a good movie? How can we overcome our hesitancy and share in open, honest, noncoercive ways our hope that persons we know and care about will receive the joy of God's all-encompassing love?

We want to help teachers discover new ways to use the

Bible in teaching; we need to find courage to share our own faith journeys in compelling, honest ways. This means telling our joys and frustrations, our disappointments and wonderful surprises! It means acknowledging our doubts and angers, always remembering that God loves us in spite of our unfaithfulness.

Faith-sharing is never seeking "to pull others up to our level"! Rather, it is our invitation to others to join us in experiencing the forgiveness and love of God through Jesus Christ. Whatever our gifts and faults, God loves us as much as, but no more than, any other person. Together, all are called to receive God's love and be graced by God's forgiveness! Wherever we are on our faith journey, we can walk the road with others. Together, we will continue to be and become faithful disciples of Jesus Christ!

4
Teaching and Learning with Older Adults

By being aware of the needs of older adults, teachers will avoid the pitfalls that block effective learning with and for these persons. By understanding the hopes and concerns of learners, teachers will be more responsive. Our goal is to involve older adults in the total planning/teaching/evaluating process.

PLANNING LEARNING EXPERIENCES

Christian education is, by its very nature, relational. Jesus modeled this in powerful ways, as he addressed persons *where they were*. Think, for example, of the Samaritan woman at the well (John 4:7-30) and the man by the pool at Bethzatha (John 5:1-9). Jesus begins the conversation where persons are; Jesus takes into account their life experiences.

In planning teaching and learning experiences, we should begin where persons are in their own life journeys and build on their life experiences. Nothing is more threatening than encountering something that seems entirely foreign. Older adults have a rich range of life experiences on which to build all our teaching and learning planning.

We should strive to use mental pictures and images as a beginning point, rather than some abstract concept. We know that involvement and retention are improved when we do this. Using concrete examples and applying what we learn to real-life situations enhances the teaching/learning experience.

Pacing is important when we work with older adults. It may take older adults slightly longer to deal with new material, but they are able to master it. We need to develop a schedule that allows flexibility and lets the group set the pace.

We know that older adults are bothered more by distractions than are younger persons; therefore, we must be sure the setting is as free of distractions as possible. We also need to be clear about the focus of the task.

Psychologists tell us that verbal skills are the least susceptible to decline in old age. This means that we ought to seek to enhance verbal communication, taking into account the sensory losses that come with aging. By speaking slowly and distinctly, by facing those to whom we speak, and by being sure that background noise is eliminated, we can provide an optimum setting for learning.

Finally, we need to be attentive to ways in which what is being done can be applied to everyday living. Learning that is problem-centered is valued most by older learners. They tend not to participate in learning that does not have meaning for them in the present.

CREATING A LEARNING ENVIRONMENT

Persons who have trouble hearing or seeing may stay home. When there are two flights of steps to climb or a dark parking lot to cross, the effort to get to church may seem too great.[1] Planning appropriate times and places for classes and arranging the room are as important as choosing good materials and planning the teaching/learning sessions.

One simple thing we can control is the *location* of the class. We need to avoid stairs whenever possible, see that the meeting space is close to restrooms, and provide comfortable chairs. Many older persons have difficulty with lounge-type furniture that is soft and low. Chairs with sturdy arms are aids for persons who need support to stand up.

The location should be accessible by public transportation and/or have adequate parking that is close and safe. Having a "space" for which a group feels some ownership can be an asset, although that is not always possible.

Room arrangement is an important consideration. The task

that the group has and the physical needs of the particular group must be considered.

It is also important to consider the personal histories of the persons in a group. While my own training and experience resists putting chairs in rows and having the teacher/leader at a desk in the front of the room, I know that there are some groups of older adults for whom this seems right. If a class has a long history of doing things a certain way, disruption is probably not a good thing.

Consider the group's goal and the methods members will use to achieve their goal; then arrange the learning space to provide a high level of comfort so that group members may achieve their goal.

The sight and hearing losses of some persons require that we provide good lighting without glare and adequate acoustics with minimal background noise. Arranging the room to allow persons to see speakers' mouths may be helpful.

Drafts may bother some people. Air conditioning that I might consider wonderful on a hot summer day is apt to be too cool and too drafty for many older adults.

The best way to create an inviting learning environment is to ask some of the older adults in the group to take responsibility for helping to determine the location and for arranging the room. The whole group might be given an opportunity to make adjustments in the setting as time goes on.

TEACHING TOOLS FOR GROWING CHRISTIANS

We have been talking about invitational teaching. Let's think, now, about invitations.

An invitation is, by its very nature, dialogical. There has to be someone to invite; there has to be one who invites. The two must understand each other. That means that there needs to be a clear statement of what one is invited to do. The person who is invited needs to be able to check to be sure he or she clearly understands the invitation. He or she may need to suggest an alternative: "I'm sorry, I can't come on Tuesday. Would it be possible for me to come on Thursday instead?"

Invitational teaching is always dialogical. It invites persons to share in a faith journey. It recognizes the validity of each person's story and invites each individual to join with others—teacher and other learners—in seeking to make meaning of life and death and to discover and deepen a living relationship with Christ Jesus.

It is absolutely essential that those invited "understand the invitation." We must use language that is understandable and that does not turn people off or make them feel as if they are in a foreign land. Using theological language or biblical images that are outside the experience of persons is not a good place to begin.

Dialogue requires that we be willing to listen to other points of view.[2] It requires us to be honest and accepting of others.

Thomas Groome[3] suggests that Christian education is a process that brings persons' own stories and visions into dialogue and interaction with the *Gospel Story and Vision*. When our own life experiences intersect with the gospel in relevant ways, growth in faith and discipleship can result.

What are some appropriate methods for engaging persons in dialogue? How can we help them bring their own life experiences and questions into contact with the Christian gospel? We have already considered the necessity of using approaches that are honest, that accept and respect persons as they are, and that are dialogical rather than manipulative or predetermined.

We need to consider other questions before we determine what methods we will use. Do the methods build on the strengths of teachers and learners, while minimizing their weaknesses? Are they appropriate, given the physical, psychological, social, and financial circumstances of all concerned?

For example, a movie that addresses issues of life and death in a powerful way might cost more than the group can afford. It is also possible that the sound track might not be loud enough for persons with some hearing impairment. We must give these matters consideration.

No method should be used to the exclusion of all others. Variety is important as we plan teaching/learning experiences. It is helpful to ask: "How can we best achieve our goal? Are there reasons that this particular method should not be used now?"

The following methods may be used effectively with groups of older adults:

Lecture is sometimes given a bad name. There are times, however, when lecturing is the best way to communicate. If one person—who is a good communicator—has information that the group needs to be about its task, then lecturing can be an efficient and effective way of transmitting information.

In addition to sharing information, lecture can be used to motivate and inspire others. Older adults grew up in educational settings where lecture was often used, and they may be more receptive to this approach than are many younger persons.

Once a group has basic information and is clear about its task, *discussion* can be a helpful tool for clarifying and moving toward a decision about what ought to be done. Planning for discussion is important. Working on questions that will help a group progress toward its goal is necessary. Discussion that is a sharing of ignorance or that is unfocused is not productive.

Media presentations (for example, films, videotapes, audiotapes, slides, charts, and diagrams) can help persons share a common experience that will enable them to move toward their goal. Whenever you use media with older adults, pay special attention to lighting, clarity, and sound volume and quality to ensure that persons with sensory losses are able to hear and see. It is generally advisable to use media that make use of more than one sense to enable older persons to compensate for any sensory losses. This means that videotapes are more desirable than audiotapes, and commentary is helpful with charts or slides.

Storytelling is a wonderful method to use with persons of all ages. Older adults are often good storytellers and ought to be encouraged to use their gifts when it will help the group move toward its goal. Perhaps having grown up with radio helps older adults use their imaginations in creative ways. In any event, storytelling can often help persons "feel with" and "experience" situations that are outside their experience. Using open-ended stories can be an effective way of stimulating discussion on significant topics.

Demonstrations can help older adults understand abstract concepts. They can also help persons follow complicated directions as they learn new skills. By being sure persons can see and hear and by checking often for feedback to be sure the pace is appropriate, you can make demonstrations a helpful teaching tool.

Hands-on-experience is hard to beat. Persons of all ages learn best by doing. We know that while we remember only 10 percent of what we hear; in general, we remember 90 percent of what we do! Being able to learn by doing (with appropriate supervision and encouragement) greatly enhances persons' self-confidence. They may find they can do things they never dreamed possible.

Role-playing allows persons to explore a wide range of issues and ideas without making a commitment or feeling judged or outside the acceptable group norms. Many older persons are wonderful at portraying teenagers, adult children, outcasts, biblical characters, and others.

Keys to successful role-playing include being sure not to typecast persons, choosing outgoing persons who will be good models for the first experience, clearly delineating the situation and the roles to be played, and stopping the experience for group input before it "runs down." It is often helpful to ask the characters how they felt. Sometimes it is desirable to do the same situation more than once and to let different persons play out the scene before having the group discuss the issues, possible options, and relevance to the task at hand.

Simulation games can help groups experience a wide

range of situations.[4] Careful preparation by the leader is necessary. It is also important to have several people answer questions and assist participants. Simulation games provide structure and a setting that allows persons to mimic real-life situations in a safe environment.

Small-group work is a good tool for teaching older adults. Breaking a larger group into groups of two to five persons and giving these small groups clearly defined tasks allows persons who will not talk in a larger group to participate more fully. It is possible, however, that some older adults will want anonymity and will not want to participate in small groups. Providing persons with choices about groups and tasks is generally helpful.

Liturgy and ritual acts are valuable ways of helping older adults focus on certain topics or experiences.[5] For example, ritual celebrations when persons retire can help them affirm the work they have done and move on to other meaningful experiences in the community of faith and in the world.

The marriage ceremony of two widowed or divorced persons ought to acknowledge the couple's desire to blend their families. At the same time, the ceremony should honor the deceased/divorced spouses in a way that will create a loving environment for the new family.

No teaching method is so good that it should be used to the exclusion of others. Persons (old and young) learn in different ways. Some persons need concrete, hands-on experience to learn best; others are highly verbal and thrive on discussing every issue. Know your group. What works well with some groups will not work with others. A variety of excellent resources is available that provides additional ideas about methods to use when teaching adults.[6]

Methods for teaching older adults in the context of a faith community must be multidimensional and interactive. They must take into account the life stories of the learners and the teacher, as well as the *Gospel Story*. How your teaching helps persons focus on the intersection of stories and Gospel Story and how it helps them discover the connections among themselves is what Christian education is all about!

Our task is to be engaged in inviting others to grow in faith. Because Christian education involves persons in a lifelong journey, the invitation we offer is never a once-for-all offer. Rather, it is an ongoing invitation to share in the fullness of life, to grow in love and understand, to become more whole as persons, to know that God loves all God's children and to understand that discipleship requires us to seek and learn and grow and change as we share our journey with others in a community of faith.

EVALUATION

It was tempting to include *evaluation* as one more teaching methodology because, in a real sense, that is what it is. But there would be the danger that it could slip by unnoticed. Evaluation is one method that we cannot do without!

The teaching/learning process is shortcircuited whenever we fail to include evaluation in the ongoing process of planning and teaching. Learning occurs when persons change. We can change the way we think and organize our view of the world; we can change the way we do things; we can gain a greater appreciation for persons or experiences. Our attitudes and values and feelings can change; our behavior can change.

Learning is not always positive. Persons can "learn" to be less tolerant and more prejudiced. They can "learn" to trust less and to share less of themselves with others.

Our task is to engage the group continually in evaluating what is happening in the teaching/learning experiences we have. We need to seek ways to discover how much and in what ways we are changing.

David Peterson maintains that useful evaluation is possible when planning and teaching includes at least three components: (1) clear and specific needs have been stated, so that we can assess how well these have been addressed; (2) the objectives the group has set are specific and measurable; and (3) tasks or activities have been completed, or issues resolved.[7] Obviously, planning, teaching, and evaluating are closely related.

Evaluation can easily miss the mark! For example, it is easy to count participants and to determine the dropout rate. We can determine how much money a program cost and how much staff time it took. We can even give pretests and post-tests to ascertain how many facts persons learned; and there is some value in knowing these things, but productivity is not the only measure of human worth.

When we engage in teaching and learning with older adults in the church, we deal with matters of consequence: whether persons were challenged to grow in their understanding of what it means to be faithful disciples, whether or not persons experienced affirmation by being loved and accepted, and whether or not persons' spiritual well-being has been enhanced. Such issues cannot be judged with an evaluation form at the end of class.

The changes that occur during an educational offering are not of equal value. Weighing the value of the learning (change) that has taken place is difficult but necessary. How many hours a group spent studying Paul's letter to the Ephesians is less important than the way that group has come to understand what it means to "get rid of bitterness" and "anger" and "hateful feelings" (Ephesians 4:17-32) when they deal with painful divisions in the church!

Teachers should always begin their planning by evaluating what has taken place in the group already. Questions such as the ones that follow should be the object of reflection, prayer, and (when needed) consultation:

> What are the needs and goals of each one in my group?
> What are our group goals? Have they shifted? If so, how?
> Can the meeting time and/or place be changed to make the experience more satisfying?
> What resources will help us reach our goals?
> What methods will best enable us to move toward our goals?
> How can I best involve the group in the planning/teaching/evaluating process?

Do group members have special gifts which could be used to help us reach our goals?

Do any group members have special problems or needs that should be addressed in some way? If so, how can both the individual and the group be helped?

Careful planning that includes ongoing evaluation enables us to be sensitive to the group and flexible in our teaching. "Winging it" is never desirable! Being free to "throw our plan to the wind," when the group process requires it, is a gift of the Spirit that grows out of careful, prayerful planning!

Evaluation, as it has been experienced by many older adults in school and work settings, can be threatening. An evaluation that focuses on the members of the group and their accomplishments can cause unnecessary anxiety.

David Peterson helps us when he suggests that the primary goal of evaluation involving teaching and learning with older adults ought to be to help the group to assess both individual and group needs.[8] How do they feel about the process? How is their living and their ability to make sense of life being helped (or hindered) by the content and process of the group? How can the setting/process/content be changed to meet their needs?

Teaching without evaluation is like playing baseball without bases, umpires, and a fence around the outfield! Be clear about personal and group goals. Goals do shift and change; that is appropriate and may be desirable! But, if lifelong learning is to be the best it can be, we need to know where the bases are, what is considered fair play, when we have achieved our goals, and when it is time to start another inning.

5
Planning to Teach

Perhaps you have been asked to teach a group of older adults in your church or community. "Why me?" may be one question you asked yourself. No list of "desired qualities" is ever complete; but there are some qualities which will, in general, be assets for those who teach older adults in the church.

TEACHERS OF OLDER ADULTS

Age is not a factor—except that being older yourself can sometimes (though not always) be an advantage. *Amount of formal education* is certainly not a criterion. I have seen successful teachers with a fourth grade education and others with doctoral degrees. I have seen "not so successful teachers" in both categories, too.

Here are some qualities that I believe will stand persons in good stead as they teach.

> Know and trust God!
> Love Jesus!
> Be growing and learning in your own faith journey!
> Be a good listener—sensitive and caring!
> Accept your own aging!
> Be trustworthy—accepting persons as they are without judging them!
> Be open to new ideas and other points of view!
> Expect to learn from and with your students!
> Be willing to try new methods—risking failure!
> Be willing to laugh at yourself—have a sense of humor!
> Be prepared, yet flexible!
> Develop skills for empowering others—This means you don't have to have all these qualities and do all these things yourself!

Recognize that process is as important as content!
Learn to deal skillfully with those who would block the group process!
Be willing to say, "I don't know! We'll have to struggle with that together!"
Pray for and with your co-learners!

AN OVERVIEW OF CURRICULUM RESOURCES

John Wesley once said, "The world is my parish." In another sense, the whole world is a resource for teaching and learning materials. There are many and varied books, films, resource persons, opportunities for hands-on experiences, and visits to places and institutions that can help us focus on our learning goals. We need to be on the lookout for people, places, and things that can help us grow in faith.

We will look briefly at some of the printed resources provided by The United Methodist Church to aid groups of older adults in their faith journeys. There are, of course, many other resources provided by both religious and secular sources.[1]

Two books published by Abingdon Press deal with aging: *The Desert Blooms: A Personal Adventure in Growing Old Creatively* by Sarah-Patton Boyle (1983) and *Full of Years: Aging and the Elderly in the Bible and Today* by Stephen Sapp (1987). These books are especially useful to teachers of older adults.

For the classroom, older adults may want to discuss their images of aging. A useful guide for such discussion is *The Gift of Maturity: New Images for Older Adults,* edited by Chester E. Custer (order no. 4310C, Discipleship Resources). Older adults from varying walks of life express their image of growing older. Group participants are asked to react to these images and identify their feelings about aging.

Thinking back to the categories used by the Shepherd's Center may help us as we consider goals for groups of older adults in the church.

Life maintenance goals often require making use of com

munity resources beyond the local congregation. Adult education offerings provided by hospitals, mental health centers, and school systems, as well as programs offered by churches, may help persons cope with budgeting resources, fuel assistance, nutrition education, and food stamps or meals on wheels. Often, one-on-one assistance is required to aid persons with these needs; their LOAD is so great that they may have no MARGIN for learning in any formal sense.

Life enrichment needs may be addressed in a planned learning experience. Those who plan fellowship or learning groups may want to look at the Cokesbury *Forecast*, published quarterly.[2]

Life reconstruction needs often cause persons to re-order their lives. One resource that can help is the new Graded Press "Doorways" series: *Living through the Death of a Spouse; Living through Separation;* and *Living through Divorce*. Persons in the stage of life reconstruction also need to share their own stories. Life reconstruction involves the whole person. Caring, sharing, and being there for persons who are trying to put their lives back together cannot be overestimated. (See the *Divorce Recovery Workshop* by Doug Morphis, Discipleship Resources order nos. LA061B, LA062K.)

An excellent study resource for an older adult group is available from Discipleship Resources as part of the series, *Times of Transition. It's Your Move: Older Adults Choose How to Live* is a guide for clergy, counselors, and social workers. Older adults looking at alternative housing arrangements and extended care will find help in choosing the best services and solutions to these needs and problems. Dorothy Gager has written this guide for pastors or counselors to help older adults and/or their families work through the medical, financial, social/emotional, environmental, and self-help needs that face older adults (DR045B). *It's My Move: Older Adults Choose How to Live* is a guide for older adults, their families, and friends. This brief companion guide to *It's Your Move* should be provided as a resource for older adults and their families or friends. Use in small groups with concerned adults as they plan for their or their family's future, or use as a workbook and counseling tool when individuals seek advice and help with the needs and problems that face older adults (LA063K).

Life transcendence needs are often left to the church. We must not avoid this crucial task of helping persons make sense of their living and their dying as they struggle to achieve a sense of integrity and to avoid despair.

Exploring matters of ultimate significance may involve persons in Bible study, and there are many fine resources listed in *Forecast*. However, Bible study does not necessarily engage persons at the level of their deepest needs. Real-life questions and concerns and persons' own life stories must intersect with the biblical message if persons are to grow spiritually. They must be invited to encounter the living Christ at their points of personal questions and pain.

Some resources from Discipleship Resources that may help older adults find connecting links between their own life stories and the gospel include *The Meaning of the Warmed Heart,* by Donald English (DR050B); *Portraits of Christ in Scripture,* by Robert Wingard (DR047B); *Life Begins at Christ, Life Grows in Christ, Life Ends in Christ,* and *Life in the Holy Spirit* by Alan Walker (EV095B, EV122B, EV134B, DR036B).

Intergenerational materials and resources for the sight and hearing impaired are available. Some materials are printed specifically for black Christians—*Touched by Grace* and the *Faith Journey* series. Hispanic and Korean resources are also available from Graded Press and Discipleship Resources.

Two large-print resources are available for older adults: *Daily Bible Study,* which comes quarterly; and *Mature Years,* a quarterly magazine dealing with issues of interest to older Christians. *Our Living Bible Series Cassettes* and a number of videocassettes are also available to assist older adults on their faith journeys. Order through Cokesbury.

DEVELOPING A TEACHING PLAN

Although there are many models for developing teaching plans, persons who are teachers by profession may want to use their own designs to prepare teaching plans.

One simple approach for designing a teaching plan is to begin by writing down one overall objective for the unit. For example, if you were leading a group of widows through a six-week class, *one* objective for the first session might be "to provide a time and space for persons to tell and to listen to one another's stories about times when they are overcome with loneliness or fear." You may have secondary objectives; but you need to be able to say, "The thing I most want to have happen is . . . "

Pay attention to the setting—how is the room to be arranged? Does it take into account the physical, psychological, and social needs of the group members?

Ask yourself, "What would be the best possible way(s) to achieve the objective for this session?" Would lecture, a film, a resource person, or some other method be most helpful?

Do you need to find ways to look at alternative actions? Would role playing, small-group discussion, or research groups be helpful?

Once you have determined how to best work toward your objective, set up a timeline. Consider the time needed for group building, the amount of time needed for each activity, and time for closure. Is there an appropriate time for prayer/worship/personal sharing?

Consider including group evaluation time. While leaders need to evaluate what has gone on before whenever they plan, the group also needs to be a part of the process on a regular basis.

Because you are seeking to plan invitational teaching, you should ask: "How has this process engaged persons and invited them to make a commitment to be more faithful disciples of Jesus Christ and to act on their faith?"

A simple teaching plan should include:
- Needs of the group members
- One overarching long-term objective
- One major session objective (secondary objectives may be included)
- A teaching outline that includes...
    —a timeline with content and methods to be used
    —a process for evaluation

One example of a teaching/learning plan follows.

A Sample Teaching/Learning Plan

Audience: Fifteen members of St. Luke's Church, who range in age from 53 to 79. Six persons are working full-time; five are retired; four are widows, who have never been employed. There are four couples, three single persons, and four persons who have lost their spouses through death. Eleven of these persons have adult children.

Unit: "Living Life and Facing Death"
A six-week series that meets 4:00 to 6:00 on Sundays during Lent.
- Session 1: Death as Enemy and Friend
- Session 2: Dealing with Grief
- Session 3: Living with Losses
- Session 4: A Christian Looks at Death and Life
- Session 5: Facing My Death
- Session 6: Freedom to Live Life!

Objective for the Unit:
To explore attitudes and feelings about living and dying in light of the gospel.

*Session 5 Objective:
To prepare for our deaths in ways that will be helpful to our families and friends.
To reflect on the meaning of my life.
To explore options regarding wills, living wills, organ transplants, etc.
To plan for my funeral and burial.

A Teaching Plan for Session 5

TIME	CONTENT/METHODS
3:45	Coffee and juice are available as persons gather.
4:00	Bidding Prayer: For those who are experiencing grief and loneliness For those who are facing death For those who are seeking to reorder their lives and to live with losses For our loved ones, especially parents and children For our church
4:05	Sharing Our Obituaries (Last session, persons were asked to write their own obituaries, including what they would hope to be remembered for.) Questions for discussion: How did you feel as you did this task? What did you discover about yourself? Who would like to share what they have written? Did writing this give you any insights into how you want to live? If so, how do you want to reorder your priorities?
4:30	Issues to Consider (Handbook, pp. 1-8) Living wills, transplants, body donation (questions and answers to be facilitated by a doctor from the church)
4:50	Wills, bequests, insurance, government benefits (questions and answers to be facilitated by a lawyer from the church)

5:05	Break
5:15	Funeral and burial arrangements (Handbook, Appendix A) (questions and answers to be facilitated by a mortician from the church)
5:30	Planning a Service of Death and Resurrection (Handbook, p. 10) (questions and answers to be facilitated by the pastor)
5:50	Unfinished business; agenda setting for last session
5:55	Closing song: "For All the Saints" Sending forth
6:15	Evaluation by planning team (three members of the group and the pastor/leader) What was the most significant thing that happened in this session? What problems did we experience? What was the depth and breadth of participation? Did everyone participate? Did persons listen to one another? Did anyone monopolize the discussion?

What do we need to incorporate in our plan for next week's session?
Review the next session plan.
Assign responsibilities for follow-up on absent group members, arranging the room, providing needed resources, and teaching.
Prayer for group members.

Time used for planning is time well spent. Once you have a plan, be flexible in how you implement it. Encourage feedback from the group; provide them with opportunities to assist in revising the group's joint plan for learning.

Conclusion

We have reflected on ways to teach and learn creatively with older adults in the church. It is a task that brings rich rewards. Older adults bring a multitude of experiences, deep hurts, and hard questions to any significant teaching/learning encounter.

Those who teach and learn with older adults must be willing to be open and honest—to risk sharing themselves with the group. Older persons are skilled at sensing when honesty is (and isn't) present in a relationship.

Affirming the worth of all learners and accepting them as they are is important.

Listening to their stories and questions and guiding them as they encounter the Gospel Story so that it speaks to their situations is what we are called to do.

Inviting them to experience the forgiving, empowering love of God and to grow toward wholeness is the gift we have been entrusted to convey.

Calling them to respond to God's great love for them with acts of justice and mercy is also a part of the message we have to share.

Being co-learner, friend, confidante, and brother or sister in the family of God is part of what it means to accept an invitation to teach and learn creatively with older adults. You are invited to grow with those you teach in love for God and service to our global community.

Notes

Chapter 1. A Gold Mine of Lived Experience

1. The Shepherd's Center model was developed at Central United Methodist Church in Kansas City, Missouri, under the leadership of Elbert C. Cole. For a more detailed description, see Linda Jane Vogel, *The Religious Education of Older Adults* (Birmingham, AL: Religious Education Press, 1984), 145-51.

Chapter 2. Getting Inside God's Word with Older Adults

1. These guidelines were described by Dorothy Jean Furnish in *Living the Bible with Children* (Nashville: Abingdon Press, 1979), 24-35. While she applies them to children, the guidelines are equally valid with all who seek to experience the Bible in a holistic way.
2. Richard J. Foster, *Richard J. Foster's Study Guide for Celebration of Discipline* (San Francisco: Harper and Row, 1983), 20.
3. Ibid.

Chapter 3. Invitational Teaching

1. A brief and clear summary of the insights provided by these persons can be found in J. Conrad Glass, Jr., *Growing Through Adulthood: Can the Church Help?* (Nashville: Discipleship Resources, 1979).
2. For a more detailed description see Howard Y. McClusky, "Education for Aging: The Scope of the Field and Perspectives for the Future" in Stanley Grabowski and W. Dean Mason, eds., *Learning for Aging* (Washington, D.C.: Adult Education Association of the U.S.A., 1976), 324-55.
3. For more information on this model, see Keith Main, "The Power-Load-Margin Formula of Howard Y. Mc-

Clusky as the Basis for a Model of Teaching," *Adult Education*, Vol. 30, No. 1 (1979), 19-33. Also see Howard Y. McClusky, "The Adult as Learner" in *Management of the Urban Crisis*, eds. Stanley E. Seashore and Robert J. McNeill (New York: The Free Press, 1971), 514.
4. See Evelyn Eaton Whitehead and James D. Whitehead, *Christian Life Patterns: The Psychological Challenges and Religious Invitations of Adult Life* (Garden City, N.Y.: Doubleday, 1979), 160.
5. See The Standard Video Bible Study New Testament Series entitled the *Gospel of Mark* prepared by the RSV Project, 460 Woodycrest Ave., Nashville, TN 37210. The New Testament scholars who enable groups to grapple with the themes in Mark include Dr. Herman Waetjen, San Francisco Theological Seminary; Dr. Fernando Segovia, Vanderbilt Divinity School; Dr. John Donahue, S.J., Jesuit School of Theology; and Dr. Steven Reid, Pacific School of Religion.

Chapter 4. Teaching/Learning with Older Adults

1. The physical setting where teaching/learning takes place is as important as understanding the psychosocial needs of the learners. The biological and physical losses which many older adults experience require that we create settings which maximize their learning potential.
2. For helpful insights into the meaning and method of dialogue, see Reuel L. Howe, *The Miracle of Dialogue* (New York: Seabury Press, 1963).
3. For a detailed understanding of Shared Praxis, see Thomas H. Groome, *Christian Religious Education: Sharing Our Story and Vision* (San Francisco: Harper and Row, 1980).
4. See Dennis Benson, *Gaming* (Nashville: Abingdon Press, 1971) for information on how to create and use simulation games.
5. For a discussion of the role liturgy and ritual can play in Christian education, see John H. Westerhoff III, "The Liturgical Imperative of Religious Education," in *The*

Conclusion

Religious Education We Need: Toward the Renewal of Christian Education, ed. James Michael Lee (Birmingham, AL: Religious Education Press, 1977).
6. See Paul Bergevin, Dwight Morris, and Robert M. Smith, *Adult Education Procedures: A Handbook of Tested Patterns for Effective Participation* (New York: Seabury, 1963); Wayne Rood, *The Art of Teaching Christianity* (Nashville: Abingdon Press, 1968); Donald F. Clingan, *Aging Persons in the Community of Faith* (Indianapolis: Indiana Commission on the Aging and Aged for the Institute on Religion and Aging, 1975); Leon McKenzie, *The Religious Education of Adults* (Birmingham, AL: Religious Education Press, 1982), chapter 8; and Linda Jane Vogel, *The Religious Education of Older Adults* (Birmingham, AL: Religious Education Press, 1984), chapters 5 and 6.
7. David A. Peterson, *Facilitating Education for Older Learners* (San Francisco: Jossey-Bass, 1983), 281-82.
8. Ibid., p. 161.

Chapter 5. Planning to Teach

1. See the bibliography for resources designed to help communities of faith discover ways to engage in effective ministry by, with, and for older adults.
2. This resource is free and can be ordered from Cokesbury Service Center, P.O. Box 801, Nashville, TN 37202. There is a toll-free number which can be used to order curriculum: 1-800-672-1789. Questions regarding content, approach to teaching, and resources on a given topic or for a special needs group can be addressed to Curric-U-Phone at 1-800-251-8591.

Bibliography

The Church and Aging Persons

Anderson, James Desmond. *Taking Heart: Empowering Older Adults for Community Ministries* (A Handbook). Washington, D.C.: Cathedral College of the Laity, 1986.

Becker, Arthur H. *Ministry with Older Persons.* Minneapolis: Augsburg, 1986.

Clements, William M. *Ministry with the Aging.* San Francisco: Harper and Row Publishers, 1981.

Clingan, Donald F. *Aging Persons in the Community of Faith* (New revised edition). St. Louis: Christian Board of Publication, 1980.

Custer, Chester E. *The Gift of Maturity: New Images for Older Adults.* Nashville: Discipleship Resources, 1986. (order no. 4310C)

Episcopal Society for Ministry on Aging, ed. *Affirmative Aging.* Minneapolis: Winston Press, 1985.

Gager, Dorothy. *It's Your Move.* Nashville: Discipleship Resources, 1987. (order no. DR045B)

———. *It's My Move.* Nashville: Discipleship Resources, 1987. (order no. LA063K)

Lawson, Rosalie Jenkins. *Our Congregation's Ministries with Older Adults.* Nashville: Discipleship Resources, 1983. (order no. 4317C)

Loughhead, Elizabeth J. *Eldercare: Starting a Center in Your Church.* Nashville: Abingdon Press, 1987.

Maves, Paul B. *Faith for the Older Years.* Minneapolis: Augsburg, 1986.

———. ed. *A Ministry to Match the Age: A Report of the National Consultation of Older Adults in The United Methodist Church.* New York: General Board of Global Ministries, 1984.

Sapp, Stephen. *Full of Years: Aging and the Elderly in the Bible and Today.* Nashville: Abingdon Press, 1987.

Vogel, Linda Jane. *The Religious Education of Our Older Adults.* Birmingham, AL: Religious Education Press, 1984.